Dear Reader,

On behalf of myself and the other
contributing authors, I would like
to welcome you to the fourth Open
Door series. We hope that you
enjoy the books and that reading
becomes a lasting pleasure in your
life.

Warmest wishes,

Patricia Scanlan.

Patricia Scanlan
Series Editor

THE OPEN DOOR SERIES IS DEVELOPED
WITH THE ASSISTANCE OF THE CITY OF
DUBLIN VOCATIONAL EDUCATION
COMMITTEE.

NOTE

World Cup 2002 was a turbulent tournament for the Republic of Ireland soccer team. On 23 May, Ireland's captain, Roy Keane, was sent home after a row with the Ireland manager, Mick McCarthy. This was a major blow to the Irish team. Yet they went on to set a record for the amount of goals scored by Ireland during a World Cup finals match. What follows is Niall Quinn's diary of that tournament adapted from his newspaper column.

New Island *Open Door* would like to thank the *Irish Independent*, where these articles originally appeared.

25 May 2002

Why Roy Keane Had to Go Home

It's been an astonishing week, very hard for everyone. It's left us with heavy hearts.

As we flew to Japan yesterday morning without Roy, I looked back and asked myself, how did it go this far? I think everyone else did too.

I suppose it's wrong to dwell on it, as we have over three weeks now to make the tournament a success. As hard as it sounds, we have to try to

1

forget what's happened and look forward rather than back.

I feel gutted for Roy that he's missed the chance to show the world what a great player he is. When we played Portugal and Holland at home in the qualifiers some would say he played them on his own. I would have said this tournament was tailor-made for him. He's in the prime of his career. I expected that when they would tot up the points and the Opta Index for best player of the tournament Roy would be up there. He's a huge loss.

And after Thursday's turbulent meeting in Saipan, as long as Mick McCarthy is in charge, I don't see Roy playing for Ireland again. While I'm reluctant to give details of the meeting or refer to what was said, it was understood by everyone there that Roy and Mick could never be in the same Irish set-up again.

I suppose there is an argument to be made that Roy should have left things alone for a few days. Instead he gave interviews to two top feature writers. That was a mistake. I think he might have needed a few days to simmer down.

Roy had a bee in his bonnet for a few days. After the first set-back, when it looked as if he was going home, we were told the following morning that everything was fine. Training was good. The problems seemed to be sorted. But the article that appeared on Thursday raised questions again. It left Mick with no option. He called the players' meeting specifically to ask Roy about it.

I think he wanted Roy to say, 'Look, I was still a bit hot and bothered. I spoke under duress when I shouldn't have.' That would have been the end of it. But as we know, Roy's reaction to Mick's questioning about the article was to explode with a stream of abuse. It wasn't just about the article. That's between Mick and Roy. There was more.

I've been a team-mate of Roy's for a long time. I've seen his career develop. It saddens me to see his international career finish like this – if it is finished. I'm sorry that he's not here with us, that he's not going to play in the World Cup finals. But I can't look any further than Roy's door for blame.

In some ways, it may help the team to become stronger, but there is a void. I'd be stupid to say we won't miss him. As Mick said on Thursday, we won't miss the bad humour, the giving out, all the negative things. But we'll miss

Roy on the pitch. He's a great player, but he wasn't the ideal captain for the World Cup finals.

To a man, all twenty-two of us agreed with Mick to send Roy home. We agreed to group together and see how the matches go. If Roy had been allowed to stay, I don't think Mick would have had twenty-two players in agreement.

Mick has the support of all the Irish players here. He has earned it over the years. He is a very sincere, solid man. We used to think that as a player he was too serious. But we realise now he was cut out for management because of that.

On the pitch, Mick was a huge influence. I've never played with anyone who did the stuff he did. He barked orders out consistently, frightened the referee, the linesmen and the opposing players, while having everybody doing their job.

Off the pitch, the rest of us would head out as soon as we could, but Mick would be discussing matches and coaching patterns. We used to think, 'Oh God, put the ball away!' But now he has relaxed as a manager. Qualifying has been brilliant for him.

There was a fabulous picture in most of the papers where he had tears in his eyes. People were saying that was the first time they had seen a soft side to him. In Italy in 1990 he didn't get that emotional. When the penalties were going in, David O'Leary was crying his eyes out, as was Packie Bonner. Mick was saying, 'Get yourself sorted for the next one.'

But when we qualified – that was the first time I'd seen him show any emotion. Having missed out on qualifying for the last two tournaments, he said he knew he could do it. I think that's why the tears came.

So here we are now in Izumo, in good spirits despite what's happened. The reaction from the people here has been wonderful, so genuine and supportive. The reception at the Dome was moving for us all. It was lovely to see the Izumo people there to welcome us. The pitch at the new stadium where we trained was excellent, and we had a lively session.

I'm not surprised that Mick has gone for Damien Duff and Robbie Keane to play together in attack today. They're the first-choice pairing and are developing a fine understanding. As an Irish fan, I'd love to see them hit it off in the finals.

Being realistic, I can't see them playing all ninety minutes of three games, and if I'm the type of player needed to come on, I've got to be ready. I might be getting on, but the first person I've to convince of my fitness is myself. I feel I'm nearly there now.

The first couple of days here I struggled, but this week has been great. I won the yellow jersey for worst trainer in Ireland and had to wear it in the first training session out here, but I got rid of it. I'm not even getting a vote these days.

1 June 2002

WILL ROY COME BACK?

I felt guilty leaving Izumo. The people there were extraordinary, polite beyond words – no intrusions, no agendas. But we were so distracted this week, I'm not sure that Izumo really registered. Not for me anyway.

When I look back in years to come, I know my lasting memories of the place will be framed in room 204 of the Royal Hotel. Tied to the telephone and dead-of-night negotiations. No sleep, no peace, no resolution.

'Hello Michael, Niall again …'

The end came for me at 3.35 a.m. on Wednesday, when Michael Kennedy rang to say it was over. Roy Keane wasn't coming to the World Cup. It was finishing with a prepared statement that none of us wanted to read. So many emotions went streaming through my head. No Roy. It was horrible for him, horrible for everyone.

The hotel had fizzed on Monday night with whispers that Roy was doing a television interview for RTÉ. He was going to apologise to Mick McCarthy. A jet was waiting at Manchester airport. I knew Michael Kennedy was desperate for him to do it.

We had been in almost constant contact. Michael is probably the closest person to Roy outside his family. And he was telling me Roy was still angry, but he felt there was a chance.

Steve Staunton and I waited up for

news. But it was very unclear. I went up to the room, rang Gillian, then my parents. They felt that, as sincere as Roy was, he hadn't moved much ground. Still, he did say that he wanted to play in the World Cup. That was positive.

I went to bed but could barely close my eyes. I just stared at the ceiling. By breakfast, word began to filter down that Mick had offered an olive branch. The air tingled with intensity. Then, Mick called a meeting for half-past ten. On the way down, there was a massive buzz around the treatment room where we go for strappings. There were rumours about a private plane leaving Manchester for Tokyo.

Then Mick effectively killed the Roy Keane situation. He was holding a transcript of Roy's interview, which the FAI had secured for him. It suggested Roy hadn't done enough. Mick indicated he was going to make a statement to that effect in his press conference after training. He wanted to finish it now with the game coming up. He said he was going to leave the room and let the players decide whether they wanted to back him or not.

We knew that if we didn't back him, Mick McCarthy was gone. He didn't say that to us, but we knew it. So we had to ask ourselves the hardest question. We insisted that each of the twenty-two players in the room spoke. That was very important. And the unanimous decision was that we had no choice but to back Mick 100 per cent, to get back to football.

It was a very solemn vote. On the way to training, a few of us sat at the back of the bus, wording a statement. We wanted to have it ready for Mick's press conference. Then the whole thing blew up in our faces. Incredibly, Mick called off his press conference and our statement got released.

But that wasn't the key to Roy's decision. I was still in constant contact with Michael Kennedy. He knew the door wasn't closed. And I received a message from a journalist to ring him just as I sat at the table for my press conference on Tuesday.

I wasn't happy as I left that conference. I had been absolutely truthful, but the whole thing didn't sit easy. I went for a walk, my head ringing. I was thinking, 'We've got to make one more effort. Roy Keane should be here.'

I rang Michael Kennedy.

'Is it dead?' he asked immediately.

'Why?' I responded.

'Because I think he's starting to come round.'

Roy understood the context of the

players' statement, Michael had made sure of that. He knew that it had been made with heavy hearts. The players would have welcomed him back with open arms.

So I went up to Mick's room. Packie Bonner was there too. And for forty-five minutes we just talked and talked. We were emotional. Eventually, Mick agreed to give it one more go.

I'm not sure that he got that message across in his next press conference. The message was that if Roy just picked up the phone in the next couple of hours he was back in the Irish squad.

I rang Michael Kennedy immediately. I was throwing my reputation to the lions but I didn't care. I was delighted. I thought Roy was coming back.

But Roy decided not to come. When I got the phone call there was a stabbing sense of deflation. Every player had agreed not only to take Roy back but also to embrace him. I told Michael Kennedy this. I offered at one stage to get any player Roy wanted on the line to tell him this, if it helped. Michael said, 'No, Roy accepts that.'

But ultimately, he probably just felt that he couldn't ring Mick. People who know him can see that's the type of man he is. He believes in his principles. Michael was devastated at the end of the line, as if the decision had bled all the energy from his body. And then the press had a free-for-all.

I still haven't stopped thinking about Roy. I can't shake the frustration of how close we got. It galled me that Roy said I was doing what I did to 'protect my reputation'. If anything, I felt I had placed myself in jeopardy. But I chose not to respond because I knew how upset he was.

Then I heard and read that the senior players in the squad somehow stitched Roy up, that we had a secret meeting before the blow-up in Saipan. That is nonsense.

Bottom line, I took a gamble for Roy Keane, and it didn't work. Roy didn't apologise, and my reputation was left in question. I'm not upset with him. Some of the senior players were upset by his accusations. And the notion that we set Roy Keane up hurts. It is utterly untrue.

With all the battering we've taken mentally this week, training has been a joy. I'm normally sick of it. But it's been the most competitive training stint I've ever been involved in. We've played very physical games – everything at full pelt. There's been an edge.

It's great to click into the World Cup on the Internet and read the speculation from the other teams. It's a release to be talking about football. I mean, you get to training, walk out on that green surface and everything just disappears. God bless football I say.

I've been confused at times over the last few days, hating football and wishing Mick had picked Gary Doherty. But now, at the end of it, I realise I love football more than ever. By that I mean all football – competitive stuff or just football with my kids. I've come out of this probably loving football more than I ever did.

3 June 2002

REPUBLIC OF IRELAND V. CAMEROON

My day in the Black Swan ends with a tap on the shoulder. 'Drug test,' says the official. It's a surreal moment. One second, I'm fit to burst with emotion in a sea of green, the next I'm trooping down a quiet corridor with Richard Dunne and two of the Cameroon players.

They lead us to a room blanketed with security. They want blood and urine tests. We can hear the muffled cheering overhead, but it feels like a world removed.

So they sit us down, give us lots of water and talk us through the steps. Maybe half an hour passes before the blood is taken in front of our doctor, Conal Hooper. No sweat there – just a little pinch and then sign the forms.

The next bit is more difficult. I have to pee into a bottle while watched by a doctor from Trinidad and Tobago and one from China. Believe me, it's not as simple as it sounds. I have to close my eyes and imagine I am in a pub toilet. I think of running water. I put a hand against the wall, as you do. Then, finally, maybe ten minutes on, we have lift off. It's such an unnatural situation.

I go roaring back to the dressing-room, but the last of the towels are being loaded into the skip. Everyone is already on the bus. I feel mildly cheated, but no matter. An important job has been done.

The day had started with a team meeting. Everyone was down by twelve. We discussed routine things, such as Cameroon and their 3-5-2 system. It was nothing new to us. They did throw us a bit by playing the long ball in that friendly against England, but that's what you expect from a crafty coach. They had no intention of playing it against us, and we expected as much.

I know Patrick Mboma hated it at Sunderland when we played a long ball. Saturday's style suited him so much better.

We got to the grounds over two hours before kick-off. We walked straight onto the pitch, and half of our fans were in the stadium already. It was eerie. It brought me back to 1990. Everyone felt something at that moment. You could see it in their faces. Guys were moved.

Maybe an hour later, we came back out to warm up, and the place erupted. It was incredible. There were still forty-five minutes before kick-off, and the emotions were just surging. Everyone was talking about the crowd, marvelling at the numbers. A few of the lads spotted their families. Between the shirts, the flags and the songs, an electric current started to run through people.

I met Mboma on the field, and we wished each other well. I hadn't had the chance to say goodbye to him after Sunderland's last game of the season because he flew straight away to training camp. He asked about my testimonial and apologised for not being there. I still don't know if he's coming back to Sunderland or not. So I said, 'Hopefully I'll see you back at the Stadium of Light and you won't have scored!' So much for that wish.

After that, it was back in to deal with ordinary things – strappings, simple dos and don'ts. It felt like an eternity, waiting. Then the knock came on the door. Outside, FIFA insisted everyone stood behind a white line. It seemed another five minutes before they allowed us to move any further.

Different people take different roles at that moment. The subs are like clumsy cheerleaders, patting the starting eleven on the back and mouthing encouragement. There's almost an 'us and them' situation. We're in a different place. Then, as the eleven line up, a couple of nervous shouts go up from players just easing tension. The voices that make sense, the calmer ones, belong to guys like Steve Staunton. He's an old hand at this kind of thing. And Mattie Holland has a lovely calming presence too. In a sense, maybe it took us the first half to get used to the occasion – or to overcome it.

Their goal was a sickener. Mboma, who else? But then we came close to equalising just on half-time when Ian Harte's free kick was almost put into his own net by Rigobert Song. It would have been a lovely time to score. Then again, half-time gave us a chance to get our heads together. Someone had put two words on the clip-board when we came back in: 'No regrets'. And Mick took that as his theme. He said, 'Lads you're coming in here regretting your first-half performance. That's because you haven't grabbed it by the scruff of the neck and dictated it. You're not doing what you're able to do.'

I think Damien Duff and Kevin

Kilbane have gone on record as saying they just felt they didn't belong in that first forty-five minutes. Mattie was probably the exception. He was fantastic throughout.

But for me, the person who made the change for Ireland in the second half was Kevin. He was a new player, and he showed everyone just how good he could be. Kevin's a flair player. And I felt, up to then, he was between two stools. He couldn't decide whether to commit himself or concentrate on protecting Ian Harte. He just wasn't playing his natural game.

A few of us talked to him at half-time. Being a club-mate, maybe I know what makes him tick better than others. When Kevin runs at defences in that aggressive style, that's when he's at his best. I also spoke to Gary Kelly about trying to find him. In the first half,

Gary came out with a lot of ball. His options were Jason McAteer, who had his back to goal, or Damien, whom he was trying to find in between three big defenders. And I just felt, 'Kevin, you've got to demand it off Gary in this half.'

He did too. Kevin just started to flow, and in the end he was wonderful – Damien too. He just wanted more and more of the ball, which is a great sign. I thought he and Robbie Keane really arrived.

But, above anything on Saturday, I thought the connection between the crowd and the players was immense. And to think that people tried to throw doubt on that. Having been there in 1990 and having witnessed it in 1994, this was more than business as usual. It was special. Maybe, in some ways, the events of the last ten days heightened the emotion and stirred people.

I was putting on my knee-pads when Mattie got the goal. Mick had told me to be ready. He said he might change to a more direct style ten or fifteen minutes after the resumption. So there I was putting on the pads when this burst of energy hit the dug-out. After that, everything changed – physically and emotionally. The team just started to play. We won all our tackles, knocked the ball around freely. We found places easily that we couldn't get near before. Watching it, I couldn't help but think that when we play football like that we're a very good side.

Steven Reid came in, a guy who thought he wasn't even going to the World Cup, and made a huge impact. He just said, 'I'm going to show people how good I am.'

Saturday surely proved there's a strong unity among these guys. We have that edge to us now. Sure, we've been knocked about a little the last ten days. But, believe me, the edge was always there. The training had been fantastic.

I can't stop thinking of Robbie's shot that came back off the upright. The ball seemed to swerve in three directions.

But there were so many chances in that second half. We were killing them. And, in the end, we were unlucky not to win. I was just hugging anyone who came near me at the end. There were so many heroes.

Within a couple of hours, we were on a flight back to Tokyo. The reception of Irish flags to greet us there was astonishing. After that, we were led into a fabulous food hall where a feast had been prepared. The atmosphere was just right. The guys were feeling tired but, privately, pretty chuffed. We had a lovely couple of hours together – the players, the staff and the mayor of Chiba.

There was certainly no euphoria. News of Germany's extraordinary win made sure of that. We've just got to ensure we're not beaten by them in Ibaraki on Wednesday. That's the bottom line.

5 June 2002

BOYS WITH THE RIGHT STUFF

Life has its compensations for an old footballer in Chiba. We have the whole of the New Otani Hotel's fifteenth floor to ourselves.

Tony Hickie is the sheriff. He prowls the corridor, watching the lift doors for intruders. There's a treatment room and a kit room. And there's always some life inside.

That's where the tea arrives around half-ten at night, where everyone puts the wrongs of the world to right. We're creatures of habit in there. We get our Fig Rolls and Mikados, our Irish tea-bags, and we talk. It's a bit like Anfield's boot-room.

Except it's not just football talk. We've been together for almost three weeks now. There's only so much you can say about the beautiful game.

Mick Byrne is like old mother hen. He exists on nerves. I think he sleeps about two hours a night when he's on these trips. It's hard for him. But he's always there, and everyone goes, instinctively, to that treatment room. You stick your head in and see who's on the table. You have a laugh. Time was we used to lock ourselves away into card schools. But they don't happen anymore.

Joe Walsh, our kit-man, still thinks we're smuggling bits of kit away. He comes into rooms asking how we are, and you see his eyes scanning the place. He's trying to see if anyone's got more kit stashed away. I've news for you, Joe. It must be going missing in the laundry. We've been wearing the same stuff for the last three weeks – the last thing we'd want is to nick it.

Gary Kelly is our comedian. He has the place in tears. When he's in full flow, I often think of Charlie O'Leary, our old kit-man. Gary used to hide in Charlie's wardrobe for hours. Then Charlie would go to bed. He'd be dozing off, when suddenly this thing would leap out of the wardrobe.

Then there's Jason McAteer. He's the thirty-year-old who cannot believe he's not still twenty-three and in the modelling catalogues. The changing of the guard has hit Jason fairly hard. The lads rib him over it because Jason's a doting dad now. Life's changed. Word came out this week on ITV that Mattie Holland was voted 'sexiest Irish player'. Jason was stunned. He couldn't believe it wasn't him. Confidence-wise, he took a bit of a battering.

Today, though, the humour takes a back seat. We're playing Germany in Ibaraki. In recent days, the players have been willing this game forward. Sure, Germany scored eight against Saudi Arabia. Sure, people expect them to breeze through the group and emerge strong at the business end of this tournament. But we finished so powerfully in Nigata, the guys just want to take it on from there. We don't have any fear about this game.

The lads who were playing their first World Cup game last weekend are hungry for it now. They love what they're doing. That tension that was in the air before Cameroon is gone. It feels as if we're tuned to a higher pitch now.

Mick McCarthy talked to the media during the week about the need to shed your respect for the opposition once you hit the field. I know exactly what he meant. He wasn't encouraging disrespect. Germany are a super side. But, when you're lined up beside them in that tunnel, all you're thinking about is how you want to show the world you're better than your direct opponent, or, collectively, better as a team.

You want to have people at home talking about you the way they spoke about Paul McGrath or John Aldridge. These guys want to create their own history. Rather than stand there with fear in their eyes, they're actually thinking, 'Thank God it's someone as big as the Germans. Because now we can really prove ourselves.' That's a big change from seven days ago when we were all up in the clouds.

Of course, this is a monumental game for Steve Staunton. To reach one hundred caps as an outfield player is a great achievement. But to be still playing such a central role, to be captain, is fantastic. That's proof that Steve Staunton was one of the most important players in Ireland's history. He is up there with the greats.

And anyone who believes that good guys get nowhere will be scratching their heads looking at Steve. My first memory of him is at Finnstown House in 1988, this kid with Rod Stewart hair. He was called in for training before the European Championship finals. It's well known that Liam Brady, the daddy of us all, was playing cards and asked Steve to get him a cup of tea. Steve told him to get it himself.

That was how Steve arrived. He didn't get taken to those championships. But he was soon in the squads after that. By 1990 he had made the left-back berth his own.

Maybe questions were being asked about Steve around the start of this campaign. Was he coming to an end? Would he be reduced to the kind of supporting role I'm now playing within the Irish team? The 'Cascarino role' it was called.

But here he is right back at the coalface. He is captaining his country, leading things from centre-back and playing probably the best football he's ever played. Steve's a man with a strong commitment to team ethos. And, after that first day in Finnstown with Liam, you just knew it would never be a problem for Steve to tell Paul McGrath or Ray Houghton what to do.

I suppose we're both in a declining minority within this Irish squad – Alan Kelly too. We come from an age of card schools at the back of the bus. The young players have computers and DVDs now. It feels different.

Steve sometimes says that I might have made one hundred caps before him (I'm on eighty-eight) if I hadn't had two knee injuries in my career. I tell him he's being kind. If fit, I'd probably have managed to play myself off the team.

Since Mick took over, Steve has been cool as a breeze. He's hugely respected in the game. He's the business really – a big man still playing the biggest role.

6 June 2002

REPUBLIC OF IRELAND V. GERMANY

Sitting in that dressing-room beneath the Kashima Stadium, I couldn't help but move the dial to rewind.

I'm the old man in this story, you see. I made my international debut against Iceland in 1986. I came on as a sub when we beat Brazil in 1987. I played against England when we beat them at Euro '88. I was part of that famous trip through Italia '90. I missed US '94 through injury. Then I came back for more. But, sitting there, bedlam raging all around, my mind seemed to fill with all the big nights we've had. After sixteen years on the international trail, I'm so lucky to be a part of this.

I was one of the first out of the dressing-room, and emotions were running free. There were tears in some corners and singing in others. I think what's making this special for everybody here is our fans. It's incredible that we can be so far from home and still see that great wall of green and hear that thunder.

For me this is bigger and better than Italia '90.

Maybe we had a few more people at the games in America. But the heart these people have shown to come and support us in Japan just beggars description.

So, for us to give them a lift in

return with Robbie's late, late goal is a wonderful feeling. It's right up there with all the things that happened in the roller-coaster years under Big Jack. At one point last night, I thought we'd be carrying Mick Byrne out on a stretcher if he didn't calm down. And he's a man who has seen it all. But something special is unfolding here. You can see that in the eyes of the young lads. They're almost star-struck with the World Cup experience.

I think it's beyond question that we deserved the draw. Oliver Kahn was by far the busier goalkeeper. In fact, he showed just how good he is – world-class in my opinion. And he needed to be to make some of those saves, particularly the one from Damien Duff.

It feels good to think we've finished strong for the second game running.

It's great that we've played a class side like Germany and, but for the saves of Kahn, would have won. So, in terms of raw emotion, this must be as good as it gets.

Germany are a class outfit, as they proved against Saudi Arabia. So, to see them struggling, to see them hacking balls out of defence and arguing with one another, was remarkable. Disappointment was etched on every German face at the final whistle. They knew that we had out-fought them.

At half-time, Mick said, 'Might need you, Quinny, for fifteen or twenty minutes.' That was the way he always put it. It might be only a flick on that would change things. But he wanted me ready. That might sound like scraps to exist on for the last few months. But I like to think I've trained as well as I could. I might not have any further part to play in this competition, but I enjoyed the little bit I did.

Deep down, I knew the game had slipped beyond the ninety minutes. When they brought Jeremies on for Schneider, it was obvious that the Germans were just killing time.

Mick told me going on to make sure that Damien and Robbie stayed right up the field and that we had a good go to the finish. He didn't want them dropping deep. If the ball came up to me, he wanted bodies around. And, just before the goal, Robbie almost got in.

He's a brilliant player. It was pure instinct the way Robbie read my header. All I've ever said to him is that I try to knock the ball inside in that situation. So when the cross came in (I think from Steve Finnan) and I got my head to it, Robbie just latched onto it naturally. We're all mad about him, but after this the kid is a real star.

To be fair, everyone was a hero of sorts. Duffer was fabulous – he showed the world what he was made of. As the old-timer looking on, I'm chuffed for all of them. But I'm made up for Steve especially.

We made a presentation to him before the game for winning his hundredth cap. Stephen Reid, the youngest guy in the squad, gave a speech, and it was wonderful. It was another precious moment along the way. And who's to say there aren't more to follow.

8 June 2002

SUPPORTERS MAKE IT SPECIAL

Did you ever ask yourself, 'What is Irishness?' What is it that makes us different – culture, language, humour? I've been thinking about this a lot out here.

I thought about it especially in the early hours of Thursday morning. There was a sing-song in the hotel bar. Players, staff, families and fans were all bound together in a great din of well-being. The FAI opened a tab at the bar – for everyone. There were songs and laughter, a sense of brotherhood.

Alan Kelly nudged me. 'Could you

imagine Sven Goran Eriksson and the English boys having a night like this?'

And I couldn't. Not that England don't have their own special moments. Of course they do. But this was so Irish, so simple and unaffected. It felt like a shorthand for what we are as people. All the emotion poured out in the bar that night. The barriers were down. There were even press lads in, no problems.

But that's what makes it special. There was nothing to cover up, nothing to hide. People should know that the players had a great night with their families and fans in the New Otani Hotel. They should know it because that's part of who we are.

Gary Kelly and the boys sang a few verses in tribute to Steve on his hundredth cap. It was a bit of a mutual-admiration society, really. But that's allowed every once in a while.

Gary is one of the big singers. I think the fact that Nicky from Westlife spent two years at Leeds must have rubbed off on him. But everyone's got their own party-piece. Duffer sings the meanest 'Leroy Brown' you'll ever hear. Robbie sings 'Father and Son'. Alan takes on the personality of Elvis.

Me? A couple of years ago, I was photographed wearing a Tipperary jersey at a Munster Hurling Championship game. Some people slagged me about abandoning the Dubs. Believe me, I haven't. I'm a Dubliner, always will be. My party piece is 'The Ferryman', a good old Dublin song.

I got it out of the way nice and quickly. I sang about four verses in forty seconds and dived back into my seat.

Everybody had a go at something. Jason did a Beatles number. Out of the blue, a fan suddenly produced a squeeze-box and started playing. The place was bouncing. You can pick three or four nights in your career like that – special nights.

And I think the team deserved it. We've had enough bad nights, enough problems in our time. For me, Mick McCarthy deserves credit for showing the foresight to allow the lads to let off a little steam. The whole thing gelled beautifully, with fans right in the middle of it all. I can't imagine they'd be in with David Beckham or Michael Owen after an England game. But there they were in downtown Makuhari, arms around people like Robbie and Gary, exchanging songs. That's our way – the Irish way.

Bottom line, every one of us is as big an Irish fan as the best fan on the terrace. Sometimes the only chance we get to say that is in media interviews. But after Wednesday's game we got a different kind of opportunity. Everyone was together. Nobody got tired. It was bright when I was heading to bed. People were already going to work in Tokyo.

And, I believe, the party went on for an hour or so longer. In the old days, I'd have been the last to bed on a night like that. But I suppose Father Time is catching up.

Thursday was our day off. We all went to Disneyland with our families. I had an awful headache. The sun was belting down, and the kids wanted to go on every ride. I ended the day absolutely shattered. But it was amazing. We were so anonymous in Disney. It felt like we were in Florida.

It just felt incredible that, through all the madness the World Cup has brought us, for one afternoon we were able to step outside. Even the game the night before was forgotten about. It just felt like being on holiday with the wife and kids.

I'm conscious that I mightn't have time for a family holiday if I go back to Sunderland. I still have to see what Peter Reid has in mind. Half of me wants to play until I'm forty. The other half wants me to be sensible. I don't want to end up taking tablets to keep playing, which I've seen one or two players do over the years.

I think Sunderland are back for pre-season on 10 July. Hopefully I'll have very little opportunity to think about it between now and then. When the time comes, I'll have a good chat with Peter. But I'm not worrying about that now. Sure, it's a big decision that I'll have to make in the next few weeks. But I'm certain I'll have more important ones to make as my life unfolds.

It was a massive thing for me that I contributed to the game against Germany. I needed to remind myself, if you like, why I was out here. I'd love to have a bigger input in other games, but we'll wait and see. It was important to get off and running. You feel for the lads that don't get a game. They work as hard as anybody. Clinton Morrison or David Connolly would have been just as desperate as me to get that call when Mick decided to change it. So it's not something I take for granted.

We've been hearing about the atmosphere at home. Apparently it's the same as it was twelve years ago. But you're just wondering if it is as good as people are making it out to be.

During Italia '90, RTÉ sent out a videotape for the players before our quarter final in Rome. It showed us the extent of what was going on at home. And the impact it had was unbelievable. Suddenly we realised the full meaning of what we were doing.

There were pictures of empty streets during the game, then the same streets awash with celebrations after the final whistle. We saw the impact it was having in schools, workplaces, pubs, everywhere. A lot of the lads in this panel would have been part of that tide of emotion at home – people like Damien, Robbie and Ian. They still talk about it, about how special it was.

In some ways they'd have a better grasp of it than me. I've never been at home for a World Cup Ireland has been involved in. I even went to America, though I was injured. So it's weird trying to imagine what it's like right now.

Maybe RTÉ will repeat their 1990 gift and send us out some footage.

I speak for all the players when I say

that what has really made the experience out here for us has been the supporters. Take Ibaraki. We were playing a world superpower, Germany, with a huge population. Yet there just seemed to be little groups of fans wearing their colours. Then you go to the other end of the ground and there's a green-and-white wall, covering more than a third of the stadium. I can't describe the kind of boost that gives a team. The support of these people made it so much sweeter that we equalised. It meant that we were able to give them something in return.

No doubt the stakes will get a little higher in the days ahead. The tension might be unbearable at times. But regardless of our fate in the rest of the tournament, what we witnessed in the games against Cameroon and Germany has been amazing. Without a doubt, it's the most incredible player–supporter interaction that I've ever experienced.

That's what was happening at the end in the Kashima Stadium, when the players linked arms and just sang back towards the supporters. You don't script those things. That feeling between Irish people is very comforting.

We've shown out here we're a match for any country inclined to think that, mentally, they might be stronger. We sing light, good-humoured songs like 'You'll never beat the Irish'. But behind it is a resolve and determination that only the great teams have.

That said, now we have to push on – win some games, go further in this tournament. Yesterday was back to business as usual. For me, it was another day without the yellow jersey in training. I'm on a great run. I've trained twenty-five days now since we met up. I don't think I've trained that much since my Dublin minor days.

I was tired yesterday. I got one vote for the yellow, so I'll probably need to sharpen up a bit. The winner, David Connolly, got eight. It was a fun day in training. But the fun will wear off as the match with Saudi Arabia approaches.

We played a game of Gaelic yesterday, and guys like David Connolly and Steven Reid took to it like ducks to water.

I remember it striking me when we played a Gaelic match last year how Dublin have missed out on the talent of guys like Thomas Butler and Brendan McGill, who are at Sunderland. I got the same feeling watching Damien and Robbie yesterday. They would be impossible to mark. At one stage, Damien caught the ball and turned. It was like Jason Sherlock at his best. Mind you, he drove it wide!

I think the fans at Inage Park enjoyed it. It's important to lighten the mood every now and then. We have to be at our peak against Saudi Arabia next Tuesday. To endure a heavy session with tired limbs would not have been the answer.

Last night was the first night I sat down to watch a full ninety minutes of football in this tournament. And what a big win for England. If I'm honest, I thought they would struggle in their group. So far, they've done better than I expected. But, then, counting chickens is not to be encouraged at the World Cup finals. Not for England, and certainly not for us.

11 June 2002

SEIZING THE MOMENT

It was just like old times for me in the muggy heat of Chiba yesterday. The squad's resident geriatric pretended he was young again. I loved it, too. It's maybe the first time in eight years I felt confident enough in my body to pull on the goalkeeping gloves.

It was a simple challenge. Two thousand yen each, and they had to score three penalties. Mick was a bit worried, and I could understand. The British captain, Emerson, had hurt a shoulder trying to save a penalty in training. But I assured him that the new, re-energised Niall Quinn was more agile than Emerson was. Mick smiled but didn't look convinced.

Anyway, it was nice to know an old man can still make a profit on the training ground. Two of the lads, Alan Kelly and Robbie Keane, broke even. The other seven took the bait and lost. I was fourteen thousand yen in the black. Please God I'll be using it to buy a celebratory drink tonight.

This is a strange game for us, as the onus is on us to win. All the positive energies that have come out in the last ten days or so have brought us to this cliff edge. We've got to get ourselves on to the next level now. We have to score at least two goals, something no Irish team has ever done in a World Cup finals tournament. But history is unimportant here. What matters is the emotional spark within the squad, the sense of unity. We believe utterly in what we can achieve in Yokohama today.

Robbie Keane has had a taste of what it's like to score in the World Cup finals. And the beauty of Robbie Keane is that, in his eyes, that's just a beginning. He doesn't look on his goal against Germany as any kind of destination. He believes he is only starting. His attitude is 'Great, now let's see how many more I can get!' And Damien Duff is overdue a goal. He's played hard here so far, and he deserves a goal.

We've been thinking a lot about where we can hurt Saudi Arabia, where we might get goals. But there has to be some balance too, as they are a dangerous team on the break. They showed it against Cameroon, who nearly came unstuck against them once or twice.

So, while everyone is thinking of driving forward, of playing an attacking game, common sense has to apply too. It's so vital that we don't concede a goal. I believe that if we can come out of Yokohama with a clean sheet, we'll have done enough to get us to Korea.

Last night, before dinner, we watched a video of the Saudis. It brought home to everyone just what they can do on the counter-attack. It was good to see, because all the talk has been about where the goals are going to come from. It's been said, mainly because of the German game, that they're weak in the air. Some people imagine that this is the way to attack them.

But there are more strengths to the

Irish game than just dumping hopeful balls into the opposition box. As players, we believe that we can create chances, score goals. My role will be the same as in Ibaraki. I'll come on, I imagine, only if things aren't going our way.

But I think that for the first hour we'll be sticking to what's got us here. That is playing lovely, positive football, with Damien and Robbie making runs, bringing other people into play. Why change? It's the correct way to play. It's the way that has brought us success. I've never been under any illusions about my role in all of this. I'm there only if Mick feels the need to change it.

As a pro, I hope I'm not needed today. But as the egotistical glory grabber that I quietly am, I would love to be the one that comes on and gets the goal that puts us through. But that's only dreaming. The reality is that we've got to get behind the eleven who start. Believe me, there'll be no regrets from anybody if we qualify from an ugly own-goal. This is all about us and what we can do to an opposition. It's new territory for us in many ways because we've never had it in our hands like this before. It's exciting. Questions have been asked of this squad from the first qualifying game away to Holland. And we've kept answering them, but this is a brand new question.

And these guys are desperate to give the Irish people the right answer. I think the Saudi's result against Germany was a freak one. Once the first couple of goals went in, their heads dropped. Against Cameroon, they looked a nation that was worth its place at the World Cup finals. They showed far more character, far more belief in themselves. So we expect a very tough game.

If I am needed, at least I know I'm in good physical shape, the best I've been in years. Saudi Arabia are, of course, out of contention. How that will impact on them is difficult to anticipate. They might start knocking the ball about, enjoying the occasion more than they did the other two. The pressure is clearly on us, and sometimes that creates anxiety and tension.

I know all about that from the year we've just had at Sunderland. We played on tiptoes almost through the season. And that detracts from your performance. We've got to be careful not to allow that to happen here. We've got to go out there with smiles on our faces saying 'Yeah, bring it on', not 'Oh my God we have to do something that we're not used to doing!' There's a desire in the team to bring this further now. It is a game that brings to mind the 1990 clash with Egypt in Palermo. I was probably the only one in Ireland who benefited from that afternoon. After that game, Big Jack decided to leave out Tony Cascarino.

As a result, I got into the team and stayed there right up to the Holland game last September. In one sense, then, Egypt '90 doesn't hold the bad memories for me it might for others. But it did serve as a reminder that you need to be tactically shrewd to overcome opposition in a situation like this. I think we might have been guilty back then of thinking we were going to bombard Egypt. They were a small team, but they coped with us and were unlucky not to win.

So we must all be guarded, even the fans, against the fact that the Saudis could make life extremely difficult for us. It wouldn't take a huge improvement from them to do that.

Still, with the force of the Irish supporters behind us and with knowing what it means to each player out here, I think we can all push forward and grab this opportunity. The reward is huge, but I dare not look any further.

12 June 2002

REPUBLIC OF IRELAND V. SAUDI ARABIA

Lovely moments just keep on coming here. Imagine a kid in a sweet shop who's just been given freedom of the premises. I saw that kid last night in Yokohama. His name was Damien Duff. He'd just scored and was running back to the half-way line, and his face was frozen in the sweetest smile. 'What a feeling,' he was yelling. 'I can't believe this feeling.'

The joy within the team when Damien scored was so strong.

Everyone just wanted to put a hand on him and show their appreciation. As the old codger, I was too tired to run over to the far side of the field with the rest of the team. I wanted to save myself for the last ten minutes. But what a moment.

Damien had a very tough time in the first half. I thought the Saudi's back three went for him every time, playing man and ball together. And it's the one part of playing as an out-and-out striker that he is still getting used to, getting your ball with your back to goal. With Blackburn, he plays primarily on the wing. So he found it difficult. But once he got himself free on the left, he looked absolutely world class.

A different pressure to anything we've experienced came on us in this game. It was a hard game for us. The first half was not enjoyable. We looked uncomfortable, and Robbie's goal should have settled us. But it felt similar to Macedonia, that awful night in Skopje when we seemed to regress a little, having taken the lead. Maybe we're better when the opposition scores first.

Emotions in the dug-out were high during that first half. Having got the goal, there was a sense that we would assume control, knock the ball around, carve a few openings. But it was the opposite. We got nervous, allowed them to get behind us, and we were on tenterhooks at times.

The theory beforehand was that a 1-0 half-time lead would be perfect, that we would stabilise from there. But it didn't feel like that at all. We knew we were lucky to be a goal up, so Mick decided to change it for the second half. We became more direct, and Damien suddenly found space out on the left. I thought we were full value after that. I know the Saudi keeper won't be happy with our third. But in terms of how we dealt with the goal requirement of the night, in terms of the general pulse of that second half, I thought the score didn't lie.

It was difficult for Harty, having to come off. It's strange. I've replaced him twice now in successive games, yet his left foot is better equipped to find me than any other. But that's football. Harty simply gave way to tactics. I know he'll be a bit disappointed, but looking back, you can't really fault Mick McCarthy.

Didn't Robbie look so hungry? He scored another goal and, generally, made them nervous. It's all systems go up in the front line for himself and

Duffer. I'm happy to come in and help them when I can.

I had a few chances to get a goal myself. The volley? I think that would have been the best goal I'd ever scored if it had gone in. I hit it well, just a little wayward. And I had another chance that got trapped under my feet. I probably should have blasted it rather than think about the slide-rule. Who cares? I think we can go and enjoy our game in Suwon on Sunday now. The draining pressure that applied last night is now, effectively, gone. Sure, there's a building pressure to keep going, to get to the next round. But it's a different kind of energy.

Last night's game was a must-win situation from a favourite's perspective. That made things difficult for us. And it showed because, for some reason, we don't perform well in those situations. We're better off being the under-dogs, when our spirits tend to kick into overdrive. I think the game approaching will suit us.

I had a lovely view of Gary Breen's goal. The composure he showed to flick it in with the outside of his boot was breathtaking. He has been a rock for Ireland over the last six years. I remember him in the under-twenty-ones years ago, when we used to have training matches. I hated playing against Gary. He was always so committed. He thinks deeply about the game, about himself and his contribution to the team. So he really deserved that goal.

We can only imagine what the scenes were like at home. When Mick came back into the dressing-room afterwards, I think he captured everyone's mood. 'The only thing wrong with this,' he said, 'is that we're not at home to enjoy it.' The dream would be to fly back to Dublin for the night and fly back here twenty hours later. I'm sure we'd all take that option if it were available, regardless of fatigue.

In the meantime, what a night! Someone pointed out afterwards that I was last off the field, just as I was in Ibaraki. Maybe it's no coincidence. I'm just savouring these moments. I'm conscious that each game could be my last in an Irish shirt. And I don't want to let it pass me by. Roll on Korea.

15 June 2002

KOREA

Suddenly, the world is coloured red. I strolled down towards Seoul's city hall after dinner last night and saw the proof. Red people, red streets, red hysteria.

The noise was a magnet. Building and building from lunch-time, it just drew us in. Professional football can be such a cynical world, a 'seen it all, done it all' existence.

But last night just blew the bulbs in my head. It looked like a million Koreans had gathered in the centre of the town to watch their game with Portugal on big screens. Everyone was wearing red. Everyone was waving a Korean flag. It reminded me of Dublin and the homecoming of 1990 – except much bigger. We ambled back to the hotel and watched the game with the sound turned down. A wave of voices rolled up off the street. We could have been sitting on the centre-circle at Incheon.

For me, the World Cup grew to another dimension here. It just shows how first impressions can be lies.

I got off to a bad start with Korea. It seemed such a different vibe to Japan. I sensed it the moment we touched down at Seoul airport. There were none of the welcoming smiles and the sense of occasion that so humbled us at Izumo. We could have been forgiven for thinking that we were playing behind the old Iron Curtain. Customs were slow. The bags were checked again and again. The first person we met was one of the armed guards.

Things are different from Japan. We had a snooker table and dart-board in Chiba, but here the snooker table and dart-board are in the Irish bar downstairs. And I doubt Mick would be too happy with us spending our spare time in a bar.

Anyway, snooker, darts, welcoming parties – who needs them when you're in the last sixteen of the World Cup? At this stage, we've had a hard four or five weeks, so the priority is rest. One or two are still going out to the shops. But we realise it's now game-on.

To be fair, I always knew there was a lot more to Korea than soldiers and stern faces. I've met Irish people who live out here, and they all like the place.

I met a guy from Galway who has lived here for a while. And he insisted that South Korea is known as the 'Ireland of the Orient'. He said that the historical similarities between us are striking. The Koreans have a similar sense of national identity to the Irish.

This is said to be the one place in the Orient where people like to go out and have a pint. They are, actually, a very friendly race.

The lobby of our hotel here is like the concourse of a train station. It's so different from Chiba where everything was relaxed and you could walk down to the beach. In Japan, there weren't hordes of people flying around the place, oblivious to us.

Six or seven national teams have been based in Seoul, so we're just part of a general sound-track. That suits us because we're on more serious business now. I think you can feel that mood around the place. One of the lads commented after Thursday's press conference that we seem to have accumulated a large number of extra journalists. It's as if we're an attraction now that we aren't in the group phase.

There's been a business-like edge about the squad since we touched down in Seoul. That's understandable. When the stakes get higher, you have to let go a lot of the fun. Mick did allow us to relax and have a couple of drinks on our first night here. But it's serious now. Spain in Suwon tomorrow. One of the hardest draws imaginable.

I have mixed memories of the Spanish. I remember playing them in Lansdowne road in October '93 and not getting a kick. That was the day they won 3-1. John Sheridan scored a late goal to bring some sense of respectability to it. It proved an important goal, because, in the end, we qualified for US '94 on goal difference. But Spain out-played us that day in Dublin. I think Jack played just one up front, and our team didn't have much versatility in those days. When we were taken away from our structured way of playing, we didn't handle it well.

Yet, I remember we had gone out to Seville the previous November and played them off the park, coming away with a 0-0 draw. John Aldridge scored a very good goal that night, which was wrongly disallowed for off-side. I also had a one-on-one with the keeper. He got the slightest fingertip to my shot, the ball spinning an inch or so around the post. That missed opportunity haunted me for a long time. So we more than matched them at their place in those qualifiers, yet they gave us a bit of a lesson at ours.

Going back further, I remember a game at a different stadium in Seville. It was November '88, when I was still trying to break into the team. And a man nicknamed 'The Vulture' scored. His real name was Butragueno. I remember it because we had them on the rack. It was about an hour into the game, and the crowd was starting to turn against them. We seemed to have done the hard part. Next thing, they broke away and Butragueno scored. After that it was party time in Seville. They kicked on to win 2-0.

We won the return match in Dublin the following April. Michel's own goal gave us a critical (and famous) 1-0 victory. So there's a history there. I think they'll be wary of us.

We told people that Germany

wouldn't out-battle us in Ibaraki, and they didn't. And one thing we can say with conviction is that Spain won't out-battle us tomorrow. We believe that this show can go even further. There is no sense of awe. The over-riding vibe is 'How far can we bring this thing?'

Perhaps it is a reflection of the new, self-confident Ireland. It also helps that there's now a history of Ireland doing well in World Cups. That adds weight to the story. It means that guys like Robbie Keane and Damien Duff want to go further than the lads of '90 and '94. They watched those tournaments as youngsters on the telly. And they've been influenced by them.

Cast your minds back to when the likes of Steve and myself were growing up, watching World Cups. There were no Republic of Ireland role models. We were hoping to do as well as someone like Norman Whiteside had done in '82, or people from other countries. We didn't have our own history to chase after. And I think that's significant now. Robbie and Damien were kids in '90 and were captured by it all. And they don't just want to emulate that team. They want to go further.

You can define world class in many ways. The easiest way to define it is when you see goals like the one Zidane scored in the Champions' League final. At key times, the top players deliver special moments like that. And they do it on the big stage. Some players aren't quite ready for the top. That's what you see with players who look good in the English first division but can't hack it in the premiership. Move that right up a level to people who can do it at international level in friendlies. But, when the big games come, they can't do it.

Robbie and Damien will never be accused of that. Because they can give their all and not be dragged down by the devil on the shoulder saying, 'You're not good enough son.'

There's a huge difference between their attitude and mine at the same age. I think it's because their mix of ability and self-belief is way ahead of anything that Jack's side contained. Up to now, we've been calling it youthfulness. But I guess it's time to say it's actually class.

They are unfazed by everything here. Unfazed that other teams will try and ruffle them, mark them out of it on the pitch. Unfazed off the pitch, in terms of not falling for all the hype.

Damien is unaffected by all the fuss about him. He spends most of his time asleep. The rest of this World Cup is almost an inconvenience for him. It's kind of 'Oh no, we're not training again are we?' Yet, the magic starts the second he walks out with the team.

Robbie is active all the time. You can't imagine him ever wanting to go asleep. People forget that he has been through an awful lot. He's not yet twenty-two, and he's played for four different clubs. He has been sold, I think, for in excess of £26 million.

If anybody had a right to feel bigger than he was two or three years ago, then Robbie would be a prime candidate. But he's very much a part of what this squad is all about in terms of how we play for each other, what we do for each other.

It's so encouraging for the other guys to see somebody like him, who could easily be forgiven for standing aloof. But, being one of the lads in the squad is the most important thing to Robbie. And that's lovely.

Even though we've been together a long time, we're still as keen and hungry on the training ground as we were on the first day in Sunderland when everyone was trying to impress Mick. Believe me, guys are still trying to impress him.

We know we didn't cruise to a 3-0 win against Saudi Arabia. It's not as if we're proud of ourselves for playing so well.

Mick, to be fair, changed things on Tuesday when they needed changing. He was quite agitated at the way we were playing. He didn't allow that to get in the way of making tactical sense. And he stirred the lads at a time when we might have gone under. The last twenty minutes were very enjoyable. An imperfect win maybe, but a beautiful occasion.

No question, the butterflies will be

active tomorrow when we sit down to the pre-match meal. It's not, usually, a gourmet meal – just fuel really. Things have gone full circle here. What used to be acceptable as pre-match food in the old days is now frowned upon. Experts who think they know everything about every person now hold court. It irritates me. I have what I always have – a big banana sandwich and about three mugs of tea. Other players have cornflakes. Others listen to their club dieticians and stick to some form of pasta. They start talking about carbohydrates and my eyes glaze over. There are some people who seem to believe that, because they've eaten a bowl of pasta instead of cornflakes, they've virtually won the game. I think people have lost the run of themselves over the years. The way the game is gone in that regard is

17 June 2002

REPUBLIC OF IRELAND V. SPAIN

I have no regrets.

It's a cruel way to go out of the World Cup, of course. But something exciting has taken shape here. I may be coming to the end, but this Ireland team is going to be in big tournaments for many years to come. I have no doubt about that. The next eight years, I believe, are going to be a golden era for Irish soccer.

That's what this tournament has shown. I'm not going home lamenting missed penalty kicks. I'm delighted with myself that I had some role to play. I thought I'd seen it all with Ireland. I thought I'd seen it all in my career. But this World Cup was new territory – unbelievable. I've loved every minute. I just wish I were a few years younger.

I found it very emotional at the end, walking off knowing that my international career was over. But it's not anything I want to labour. You just take your leave and walk away.

What a way to sign off! It could have been a damp, cold night playing away to Russia, getting dumped out of some qualifying tournament. But this was unforgettable, an incredible few weeks that we all travelled through as one – fans, players and staff. Maybe it's because I'm older, I don't know. But this will bring me far happier memories than anything I've done before.

I was due to take the sixth penalty. I honestly felt that Shay was going to save from Mendieta. I was getting ready for the kick. I just wanted one more kick in an Ireland shirt. But it wasn't to be.

I was actually quite confident I would score. When they missed their fourth – and their second in a row – I thought we had them. And what a scruffy penalty it was that claimed the victory. I thought Tony Cascarino took the biscuit for scruffy penalties. A divot hit the net the same time as the ball when Tony took his famous kick in Genoa. But Mendieta's was every bit as poor. It was probably the worst penalty he's ever taken. That's life.

I know the lads who missed are hurting. But they have to look at their ages and assess fairly what they've achieved in this tournament. We've had incredible highs out here and an incredible low at the end. That's what you need to go through.

These guys became real men, real Irish heroes in this World Cup – especially the five penalty takers. Six actually, because Ian Harte is a hero in my eyes for being brave enough to take one in normal time.

These guys have to be positive now. I think the days of Ireland being happy just to qualify for a tournament are over. We're going to have far more serious intentions from now on.

Funny how informal everything becomes in the middle of the cauldron. We had a fair idea from training who wanted to take the penalties and in what order. Mark Kinsella and myself were deciding who'd go in sixth and seventh. I said I'd go sixth, and Mark laughed back, reminding me that he had actually taken one when Charlton beat us at Wembley.

There was no sense of panic, no terror. Penalties, effectively, come down to luck. We didn't get it. But no one should feel in any way ashamed.

What do you say to the poor guys who missed? Well, you remind them of perspective. When Mattie Holland came back to the centre circle he was devastated. But, let's be honest, he has become an Irish legend with what he's done over the last few weeks. He had the disappointment of relegation with Ipswich this season, but he's had a wonderful World Cup. Yes, it was a low way to finish. But I just said to him, 'Look, you're a world-class player now. How bad is that? Why be down on yourself?'

Poor Kevin Kilbane was beside himself. He had a magnificent game last night. He showed for the ball from the first whistle. Things didn't fall kindly for him, between the penalty miss and the skewed rebound after Harry's effort was parried by Casillas. But he was fantastic. Kevin Kilbane has set the standard for himself now. He's got another forty caps in him, and hopefully most of them will come at big tournaments.

Someone said afterwards there's a big homecoming planned for us in Dublin. The people have always amazed me, but never more than on this trip. I don't know whether it's because we've been so far away from home or because of everything that went on in the build up. But the power of what happened here has been frightening. If the players get a homecoming, I'll be telling them to save every memory, as it's precious.

I didn't do that in 1990, and I feel guilty for it. I was younger and, in many ways, let the moment slip by. Well I won't be letting this one slip, no matter who turns up to meet us.

We had two or three retirement parties last night. Some guys were down afterwards, others not so bad. The important thing is that people remind these players how good they are, how good they have been and how good they can now become.

Duffer? For 120 minutes, he was absolutely fantastic – breathtaking. He's one fella I'll be glad to tell my grandchildren that I played with.

Robbie? He scored three World Cup goals – four actually, if you include his second penalty. He grew up so much over here. People still talk about

91

Robbie in slightly negative terms, about it not happening for him at Inter and Dave O'Leary not playing him that much now at Leeds. But he's going back now with his chest out. Watch Robbie Keane, I say. Because he's going to be sensational. He's been a star.

And, out here, I'd say he was in good company.